SETBACK OR SETUP:
Trusting God's
PROCESS FOR YOUR LIFE

SHERITA GREEN

Copyright © 2022 Sherita L. Green

ALL RIGHTS RESERVED. This book contains material protected under International and Federal Copyright Laws and Treaties. Any unauthorized reprint or use of this material is prohibited. No part of this book may be reproduced or transmitted in any form or by any means, electronic or mechanical, including photocopying, recording, or by any information storage and retrieval system without express written permission from the author/publisher.

Unless otherwise noted all Scripture, quotations are taken from the King James Version of the Bible. All rights reserved.

Book Cover Design: Prize Publishing House

Printed by: Prize Publishing House, LLC in the United States of America.

First printing edition 2022.

Prize Publishing House

P.O. Box 9856, Chesapeake, VA 23321

www.PrizePublishingHouse.com

ISBN: 978-1-7379751-6-8

CONTENTS

DEDICATION 1

INTRODUCTION 10

WHERE YOU COME FROM DOES NOT DEFINE
WHERE YOU ARE GOING 13

MY STORY 15

MY STORY (AS A YOUNG ADULT) 32

ANOTHER SETBACK 40

DO NOT DEFINE YOURSELF BY YOUR PRESENT
SITUATION 44

REALISTIC EXPECTATIONS 49

MAJOR LOSSES 54

BACK AT IT AGAIN 58

THE PROMISE AFTER THE PRUNING 64

DO NOT DEFINE YOURSELF BY YOUR PAST 67

I DON'T LOOK LIKE WHAT I'VE BEEN THROUGH 70

I WILL BE THAT WOMAN!!! 73

CONCLUSION 75

AFFIRMATION 78

THE SCARS 81

"For I know the plans I have for you," declares the Lord, "Plans to prosper you not to harm you, plans to give you a future and a hope." -Jeremiah 29:11

DEDICATION

To God, the number one player on my team who never ceases to amaze me. Together, we did this!! I am forever grateful for Your love and compassion towards me, even in those times when I may not have loved myself.

To my parents, Larry and Rhonda, because of you two, I am. You are the best parents a girl could ask for. I have endured so much in life, but neither of you ever left my side or failed to ensure that I was always protected and had everything I needed. I pray that I have made you proud to be my parents.

To Pastor Shavon Smith, it was your prayers, your pour, and your heart that saved my life. I can remember being so deep in depression, literally ready to give up on everything. I didn't have a purpose nor a will to live. Then, the Lord led me to Daughters of Sarah, where the words *you can build on broken bones and broken bones do heal* resonated so much with me. It was through your mentorship that I was able to find myself again. This was the best decision of my life, and nothing has been the same since. Thank you for your love, sacrifices, and heart towards me.

My bestie, best friend, my rider, Sharita…..where do I start? You have been there with me my entire life. You have seen my ups, downs, fears, failures, wins, and successes. It's rare to find friendships that last a lifetime, and I am forever grateful for the bond we share. I love you to pieces, friend. Thank you for always listening, praying, encouraging, but most of all for never judging no matter what craziness I was going through. You have always been just what I needed at the moment.

To my two grandmothers, Eunice and Dorothy, who laid the foundation for me. To my Granny, Eunice, who taught me faith, grace, respect, and many more of life's greatest lessons, there's not a day that goes by that I do not think of you, but I am so thankful that I have you as my angel. Grandma Dorothy, you are the reason I have such great intellect. You taught me to read and the importance of education. I saw your passion for it, and it quickly became mine as well. I know I am successful because of both of you.

To my little best friends: A'Naya, Amani, Kalyn, Cheniyah, Shyanne, and Kaya. I love you girls with everything in me. I always tell everyone I wanted six daughters, and God gave me just that through you all. You have the world at your fingertips and can do whatever you put your mind to. Thank you for being my motivation, my cheerleaders, and my reasons to live.

To **ALL** of my aunts, uncles, cousins, family, and friends who have always believed in me and never gave up on me, your support throughout my life has been unexplainable and always what I needed to get through some tough times. Special thanks to my Aunt Tiny for always standing by my mom and helping to guide my upbringing, and ensuring my success. To my Aunt Bam, Auntie, Aunt Lynn, and Aunt Diane, who have always taken care of me in some manner. It does take a village. Thank you to my cousin, Renita (Nurse Betty), who was always there to take care of me and ensure I was fed whenever I was sick.

To my girlfriends, LaToya (my first friend), Brittainy, Mika, Amber Lou, and Amber, you girls are the true definition of friends. I call you girls out by name because I remember my days of sickness and depression. You all made sure I ate, had company, got my meds, and always had a smile on my face, sometimes sacrificing other things you could have been enjoying to make sure I was okay. I will never forget your kindness towards me. Thank you for your push!!

There are so many others that have played an intricate part in my journey, too many to name, but if you played any role, great or small, "Thank you, Thank you, Thank you!!"

FOREWORD

TRANSFORMATION – Life is a process, and as human beings, we are constantly changing, growing, and evolving. There is a saying that we are currently going through something, just came out of something, or are about to go through something. During the process, several things take place physically, mentally, emotionally, and spiritually. We grow older; we experience grief, hurt, heartache, betrayal, and growing pains. We sometimes lose ourselves, then find ourselves again. We make bad decisions and mistakes. Sometimes we learn from them, and sometimes we do not. We go through a period where we wonder exactly what our purpose is, if we are fulfilling our destiny, and even periods of uncertainty. There may even be days when we question our existence. Throughout the process, we experience all sorts of emotions – depression, regret, anxiety, and loneliness, to name a few. While we are constantly evolving and the wheels of life are continuously spinning, it's often hard to see the other side of change.

What is transformation? It is "a complete or major change in someone or something." (Bibles of America, 2022). Self-transformation occurs internally within each of us, ultimately calling us to a higher place of being. There is an alteration, an uprooting, or a change of some sort during transformation. It is a removal from your current state of being or mindset. When I think of transformation, I am often reminded of the butterfly and the cycle of metamorphosis. For a period of time, the butterfly remains in a cocoon. It has to endure a particular process before becoming the beautiful creature it was created to be.

Like the butterfly, many of us have to endure the process of transformation before we gain our wings and soar to our fullest potential. The process may be challenging and seem unbearable, but we have to endure the process to become who we are destined to be. It is at the end of the process, at the point when we think that it is over, that we evolve into a new creation. Behold, old things are passed away, and all things become new (2 Corinthians 5:17). We have to trust God's process for our lives.

If there were a word to describe Sherita, it would be "resilient." In the many years, we have been in covenant, I have watched her overcome many obstacles and come out victorious! As a woman of little words but of HUGE faith, she finally tells HER story! She has written my stories for me many times as my admin and left brain;), but now the world will finally hear the heart of a graceful warrior that I am proud to call my friend, spiritual daughter, mentee, and administrator. May the book encourage you to keep going despite the hindrances, pain, disappointments, setbacks, and losses you experience. You should ask yourself: Is it a setback or a setup during the purging, pruning, and transformation? I say setup because I know that ALL things work together for good, and weapons form, but they will not prosper. Remember, everything you have endured has qualified you not for a setback but a SETUP!

As you read this book, I pray that you will learn to trust God's process for your life and walk into your destiny!!

~The caterpillar is resting before it becomes a butterfly, and you too will find your wings.
TRUST THE PROCESS.

-Pastor Shavon Smith

INTRODUCTION

Some may say, why write a testimony? Others may say, why not just speak it? As I sit and contemplate the answer to those same questions, one thought comes to mind. Maybe God wants me to write this testimony to tell the WHOLE story. Often when individuals are moved to share their testimonies, it is through some form of prayer and praise service, witnessing, or just a motivational/encouraging moment, all of which have some form of time restraint. Also, when speaking a testimony, there is always that chance of leaving something out that could significantly impact someone else. I have felt the need to share my life's stories for many years, but always too shy and fearful of doing so. Recently, I thought to myself, "What if my story is the key to blessing someone else," or "What if me not telling my story is keeping others from seeing the Glory of God and all that He can do?" God confirmed this for me with another simple question, "What if you are My only proof for some people?" Overcoming my spirit of fear, for the Word says, "God has not given us a spirit of fear, but of power, love, and a sound mind" (2 Timothy 1:7); I am writing this memoir to communicate three things:

- Never be ashamed of what you have been through,

- Always reach for the stars, and

- If God takes you to it, He will bring you through it.

God has put me in a place where I have endured many things; to see me and all I have

accomplished, one may never even know. I write today to share not only my tribulations but also my triumphs. I hope my story touches the hearts and lives of others all to the Glory of God. Through my story, I pray that others will see Him for who He is.

WHERE YOU COME FROM DOES NOT DEFINE WHERE YOU ARE GOING

Born January 6, 1982, I am the only child of parents with high school educations. My father was a steelworker, and my mother was a waitress. At a younger age, I personally never thought I would get to see the world or even experience college life or life outside of the "country." I was born and raised in a small county with the help of my grandparents, who were a cook, a farmer, and a homemaker. At one point, I used to always look at growing up in the "country"

as a disadvantage because there were fewer opportunities than in the city. Little did I know growing up in the "country" and in "old-fashioned" households had a world of possibilities and prepared me with the skills necessary for life's survival.

Growing up in the "country," I was taught respect, good work ethic, values, morals, and what it means to be a family. I was blessed to know all of my aunts, uncles, great-aunts, great-uncles, many cousins, and even my great-grandparents. I was raised in my family church, accepted Christ, and was baptized at the age of seven. As a child, life was full of adventure. As a teenager, life was complicated. As a young adult, life was difficult. As an adult, I am reaching my destiny and fulfilling my purpose.

MY STORY

I grew up in the small town of Surry County, VA, originally residing with my mom at her parent's house, along with my aunts and my cousin, Kevin. Growing up and being raised in such a blended household, there was no lack of love or attention when it came to my cousin and me. I clearly remember being totally spoiled, and holidays and birthdays were never missed. But the main advantage of being in the household with my grandparents was the unconditional love and lessons I received while there. While my mother was at work, days with my Grandma Dorothy went something like this: breakfast, *The Price is Right, The*

Young and the Restless, and *The Bold and the Beautiful,* lunch, and a ride to Robert Little's grocery store in town (Smithfield) with her and my great-grandma, Georgette, but the most exciting part of the day for me was reading and learning to do crossword puzzles with her. Yes, I attribute my brains to my grandma because not a day passed that we did not read a book!

I became very familiar with Urgent Care at an early age. At the age of two, I was adventurous with my cousin Kevin, ran through the house, ran into the table, and burst my eye open (the scar still remains from the stitches). About a year later, I had to get stitches on my tongue (probably for crying too hard about something and biting it). Then on top of all of that, a few years later, I fell off of my bicycle and had to get stitches in my knee. None of these are too severe, but the scars still remain as a reminder that I have endured and survived. See, I was trained to be a warrior at an early age.

Setback or Setup: Trusting God's Process For Your Life
Sherita Green

When I was four, life changed a little. My parents got a home, and we now resided as a family, my mom, my dad, and I. I was new to the neighborhood and met my first friend, LaToya. Being an only child was quite challenging and boring, so I was grateful to have a friend. Weekends and summer days were spent at my Granny Eunice's house. I loved it because I had millions of cousins in the neighborhood since all of my Granny's sisters and brothers were neighbors. Here is also where I would develop my love for Christ and the church. Surprisingly, I was one of the outgoing ones, always ready for fun and to be the star of the show; singing and dancing was my thing.

I was blessed to be a cheerleader and play the clarinet in the Marching and Concert Bands as a youth. In the following years, life's trials began for me at 12. On a typical day out at the mall with my aunt, cousin, and grandma, I suddenly fell to the floor. Of course, this was attributed to clumsiness. About a week later, I fell down the steps. Then about another week later, I fell off the school bus while arriving at school. When taken to the school nurse, I was picked up by my parents and taken to my pediatrician. Upon arriving, we were notified that he was out that day, and we would have to see someone else (God always places people in the right place at the right time). After examining me and listening to my symptoms (I had started to lose muscle strength and develop a skin rash), he immediately suggested that I had Dermatomyositis, a rare muscle, and skin disease. For confirmation, I was referred to Children's Hospital of the King's Daughters in Norfolk, VA.

This was the beginning of a long, challenging journey for me. I was referred to several different doctors, neurologists, and dermatologists. You name it; I saw them because the disease was so rare. I had to endure several EEGs, EKGs, lab work, and other tests at such a young age. Since the doctors could not pinpoint the exact cause or treatment, I was admitted to the hospital for three days.

Once the doctors and neurologists confirmed the diagnosis, I was prescribed Prednisone, which caused a dramatic change in my appearance, especially the face. This was the beginning of the feelings of insecurity for me. Imagine being 12 years old and looking in the mirror, not even noticing who you are. My face had become extremely fat. I was developing the most awful pain sores and scabs around my neck. They burned, and I felt like my skin was on fire. And yes, at the age of 12, I felt like I was Job. All I could think of was how the Bible says he had sores from head to toe. On top of the dramatic change in appearance, I was also dealing with the body rash on the skin above all of my major joints and facial discoloration.

All of this proved to be way too much for me to handle, and I began to go into a shell. I was no longer the bubbly, outgoing Sherita but had transformed into a very introverted and insecure child. The doctor's visits were draining me; they constantly asked me to do things to test my strength that I thought I was not strong enough to do, which was very frustrating. I cried and cried. It made me feel incapable. I could not do what other children my age were able to do, I could not get on and off the school bus (they even offered to have the handicap bus come and get me), and sometimes my Physical Education teacher would even yell at me because he just thought I did not want to participate, but I was just not able to. I was embarrassed. I felt ashamed and often walked with my head down. As much as I loved learning, I now hated going to school. Every night I experienced anxiety about how I would get onto the school bus. Because I was so weak, I didn't have arm or leg strength, and it was sooooo hard!!! A moment that sticks out to me the most is about two years later when I was in the eighth grade. Going through the lunch line, I passed by a group of people, and someone shouted, "Ugh, she looks like she has AIDS."

I was distraught and just wanted to die. To this day, I still remember the faces and how they made me feel. I immediately begged my mother to take me to get some makeup to cover my facial discolorations (which I still wear to this day). I had to do it so much back then that it just became a part of me. Little known fact, I just started leaving the house without makeup about five years ago. That's right; it took over 20 years to become comfortable with what I looked like without it. Little did I know God had more incredible plans for me and would elevate me above everyone else. Always being studious and maintaining Principal's List or Honor Roll throughout school despite my circumstances, I was recognized before the entire school with an Academic Fitness Award from the President of the United States, who at that time was Bill Clinton.

After undergoing treatment for Dermatomyositis for four years, one day, during a routine check-up with my neurologist, he noticed a curvature in my spine. Still dealing with emotions from the previous diagnosis and side effects of the Prednisone, I just wanted to cry. Here comes something else. After making an appointment with the orthopedic doctor, he revealed that I had Scoliosis and would have to have back surgery and have a metal rod inserted into my back. At the age of 16, I was not trying to hear this. I had just overcome a significant hurdle!!

On August 16, 1998, I was again admitted to the Children's Hospital of the King's Daughters for surgery. A Harrington (metal) rod was inserted along my entire spine to correct the curvature. A couple of days after the surgery, I developed an infection, and the incision was not healing correctly, so I had to go back into surgery so they could open it back up. Once open, they decided to leave my back open for about three days so that the infection could be treated. Lying on my face for three days with my back wide open and stuffed with gauze and betadine took its toll on me, and I slowly began to sink into depression. On top of that, I started to develop fluid around my lungs and had to go through yet another procedure to have it removed. Once the surgical area was closed again, a tube was inserted to drain the fluid; I began to develop severe chills due to the morphine; I had staples from the top to the bottom of my back and was in a great deal of pain.

Being in the hospital for almost two months, the depression really began to sink in, and I had to be seen by the hospital therapist/social worker. All I wanted to do was go home. Before being discharged, the doctors had to insert a Peripherally Inserted Central Catheter (PICC) line (an IV tube that gives access to the large central vein near the heart; and is generally used to provide medications or liquid nutrition) so that I could receive medication at home. Finally, when the time had come for me to be discharged, my parents informed me that I would not be going home but to my grandmother's house, where a home health nurse would visit me daily. Oh no!! This was the last thing

I wanted. I just wanted to go home, be in my room, and see my friends. I had been away from my environment for so long and was once again depressed. Let's just say that enduring depression as a child is brutal.

During the nurse's third or fourth visit, it was discovered that the PICC line was not working correctly, so I had to go back to the hospital to get another one inserted. I had continuously been asserting that I was not feeling well and I did not like the medication, but everyone just thought I was reacting to the situation at hand. One day as I was bathing, I suddenly felt faint and passed out in the bathtub. I had to be rushed back to the hospital. The diagnosis was that I had a reaction to the medicine, it harmed my kidneys, and it was concluded that I was allergic to sulfa drugs. As a result of the infection and medication, my balance and equilibrium were totally off. I could no longer walk, balance myself, climb stairs without rails, let alone come down stairs without feeling like I was falling and needing something or someone to hold onto. I had to attend physical therapy and learn how to walk again, and work to gain my strength back in my muscles. This was not an easy feat. To this day, I still struggle with equilibrium issues, have difficulty climbing or going down anything without a rail or assistance, and my speech is sometimes affected.

While recovering from the back surgery and all of its complications, I had to be homeschooled the first half of my junior year. Returning to school, I looked like a completely different person and had lost a lot of weight. I felt I had missed out on a lot, but I had good friends. They came by to visit, helped with my medications, and even kept me informed of important activities so that I could attend, and to this day, I still have those friends.

Junior prom came, and I was somewhat excited but also worried at the same time because how would I ever get a date looking the way I did. (I'm sure I looked fine but was still dealing with the residue from the Dermatomyositis). I certainly did not want anyone to see this awful scar on my back. I became extremely self-conscious about it for fear of being picked on, questioned, or judged. I wrestled with this for years and would never wear my back out or have my hair covering it. Believe it or not, it has taken me over 20 years to be at peace and comfortable with it.

My cousin was nice enough to hook me up with a date. Preparations were in order, and I was somewhat excited, but still, in the back of my mind, I felt something would go wrong because, after all, nothing went right for me. Well, of course, it did go wrong, and my date changed his mind. This was hurtful but taught me an important lesson: never rely on someone else for validation or your happiness. You have everything inside of you that you need. If they don't like you, then that's their loss.

Despite missing half of my junior year, I was still able to come out on top. I was inducted into the school's National Honor Society, voted as Miss National Honor Society, and inducted into Who's Who of America. That year I received several awards for the highest average in several of my Business Administration classes became a member of Future Business Leaders of America. Although I could no longer participate in the band as in previous years, I was a statistician with the girls' softball team. (No doubt I am a daddy's girl, and my love for softball and football came from him).

Nevertheless, things started to look up for me in my senior year of high school. I was accepted into both colleges I applied for; I graduated 7th in my class with a 3.8 GPA. My story about graduating and overcoming obstacles was even featured in the local newspaper.

You see, it is possible to go through and still come out on top. The key is never to stop going.

Regardless of how I felt, I knew I had to keep pushing. It was rough, but I made it. Not only did I make it, but I had several awards and honors (to name a few):

- USAA United States National Honor Roll Member

- United States Achievement Academy National Awards Yearbook

- Pride of Virginia and America Achievement Programs

- National Honor Society

- Who's Who Among American High School Students

- Several academic and performance awards for ALL 13 years of schooling

Despite all I endured as a teenager, I always persevered and found comfort with friends and my church family. I can remember being as young as seven and making my way to church. I never wanted to miss a Sunday and often went alone ahead of other family members so that I could make Sunday School. Enduring so much made me want to become a motivational speaker and mentor others younger than me. I could slowly see God using me as a vessel. Never underestimate what effect you may have on others because there is always someone looking up to you. I gained a lot of my strength and determination from one of my cousins battling Multiple Sclerosis at the time. She was so resilient and graceful and had so much fight in her. I never once saw her complain or become defeated.

So here I am, little old me, wanting to make a difference in spite of. At church, I was a tutor for the after school tutoring program, I was secretary of the Sunday School, Youth Choir, and Youth Group, I sang in the Gospel and Mass Choirs, I taught preschool and teenagers in Vacation Bible School, I taught Children's Church on Sunday mornings, I did the church announcements, and even volunteered once a year to feed those in need at the community soup drive. This was when I realized that giving back and helping others is what makes me happy. During my senior year in high school, I began to see my impact on the youth, and I felt that they needed more to stay interested in church. I prayed about it, and it was laid on my heart to start a youth revival and have praise and worship before the service. It was then that I gathered a few members from the youth choir and the congregation and started the praise and worship team. We ministered and touched so many people through our gifts of song that we later became a group, "Angels in Harmony," and ministered through song at several events and locations throughout the area. What a great feeling to see a vision come to pass. Two of my close friends and I decided to start a Praise Dance ministry about the same time. We would meet every week to choreograph routines, teach them to the group, and minister at our church and other churches in the area. This sparked a very high interest with many of the girls and allowed me to become closer and be an inspiration to them. But not only was I inspiring them, little did they know they were inspiring me and keeping me alive. I always took great pride in spending time with them, even outside of church activities.

MY STORY

(AS A YOUNG ADULT)

Beginning college at Christopher Newport University was the beginning of a new chapter. After all I had been through, I had become a shy, withdrawn individual, constantly concerned about what others would say about me or how I would be perceived, and somewhat plagued by low self-esteem. Throughout college, I spent a lot of time redefining myself and finding out exactly who I was, often trying to find fulfillment in things that were not really who I was or who I was called to be. I often wondered why I still did not have a boyfriend, but I prayed and knew everything would work out in God's time.

Adjusting to college and the new environment proved quite challenging at first. However, I adapted pretty well and made several new lifelong friends. I was employed in the Office of Admissions, and life seemed to be looking up. I entered college as a Business Administration major because that was my strength, but I felt there was more to life. I wanted to help people. I wanted to be a mentor. I wanted to see everyone do good and not struggle in life. As I was doing some soul searching, I said to myself, "You need to do Social Work." This would allow me to use my gifts and bless others. To this day, I always strive to serve others and be a blessing to those in need.

People often asked why I was so quiet or never talked because I was always quiet in class and around those I did not know too well. To me, that's just how I was, but I did not feel that prevented me from accomplishing my goals. In my senior year, I took part in an internship at Head Start as a Family Services Worker. While I did very well in my job role, aced all of my papers, and did very well on all of my class presentations, I was told that it would probably always be hard for me to advance in the workplace because of how reserved I was. Of course, it crossed my mind that maybe they were right. I was constantly worried and stressed about succeeding; I even began to have anxiety attacks at one point. Though told I would never be able to excel, I earned my BA in Social Work and earned one of the best GPAs in my major. Lesson learned it does not matter what others say about your destiny or who others say you will become; it matters what God says.

After graduating from college, it was rather hard to find employment in my field. I already had a job as an Office Assistant at La-Z-Boy, so I just decided to stick with it until I found better. I excelled several times; I moved from Office Assistant to Office Manager to Administrative Assistant for the Regional Manager. While others in my role were being laid off, I was still promoted.

As I was heading to work, the job was performing some construction, so we had to park in another area. While attempting to cross into the parking lot, I slipped. In a great deal of pain, I could not move. By the grace of God, there was a man outside cutting grass who was able to get me some assistance. I was rushed to Urgent Care. After being examined, I found out that my ankle was broken, fractured, and dislocated. I had to be transported to the hospital for emergency surgery. After a two-day hospital stay, I would be coming home with seven screws and a plate and facing months of recovery. I was out of work for about three months and had to undergo physical therapy. A couple of years later, my ankle was still giving me problems, so I decided to undergo another operation and remove the hardware. I was told that it would probably never be the same and that I would suffer from arthritis later in life, but I have no problems.

What seemed to be a problem for me would later be a blessing. While friends and acquaintances all had significant others, I was just lost in the crowd. While "looking for love in all the wrong places," I decided that I would wait for God to send me someone. One day while sitting with a friend, she stated that she had someone she wanted me to meet. I said, "Okay, but is he into the church and not in the streets?" This was a must for me. She stated that he was, and we started to communicate. Some circumstances arose in our relationship, and we parted ways, but I was blessed to be in another good relationship. While this relationship was not bad at all, I just felt my heart was still somewhere else. I often wondered if I made the right decision, and there is always the "what if." I often wondered whether I should follow my heart or my mind? I am sure this is a question that many often ask themselves as well. Needless to say, I followed my heart and would find myself back in a relationship that would last over 15 years. There were good and bad times; however, as I grew older, I found myself in a place where I was no longer happy. I realized I could not be satisfied in the relationship because I was not happy with myself. Not only was I not happy with myself, but how could I be when honestly I did not even know myself. I still had so much baggage and insecurity from the childhood trauma. I was very passive and complacent and did not have a voice. During this process, I learned a few things:

1. Follow your mind, not your heart. You should not allow your emotions to be your master or make decisions based on emotion.

2. Take the time to get to know yourself. Learn what you like and don't like.

3. Know that you are important. Your feelings matter. It is good to want to satisfy your significant other, but at what cost? Are you settling for the sake of someone else's happiness?

4. Find your voice!!! Don't always be the "yes girl." If you are uncomfortable or don't want to do something, say no.

5. Never settle, thinking things will change.

6. Protect your peace at all costs!!!!

7. Never give out more than you are getting back. You cannot pour from an empty cup.

8. Find the strength to get away from mental or emotional abuse and break unhealthy soul ties.

I can't blame God for staying too long because I clearly ignored His voice and insisted on doing what I wanted. I was always told you can't obey God and He not bless you. As soon as I obeyed, I was blessed. I am still blessed beyond measure. Something that seemed to be the end of the world to me actually was not so bad after all. I did not have to go through the hassle of having a lot of heartbreak over and over again because I only had two serious relationships. I learned an important lesson to never settle for less than you deserve. Just because you feel a need to be in a relationship, it does not mean you take what you can get because, in the end, it is worth the wait. Be true to who you are.

ANOTHER SETBACK

I always knew something was different about me. I did not start my cycle until I was 15, but they attributed it to my medication and other medical issues. One day at a routine check-up at the OB-GYN, they discovered that I had Polycystic Ovarian Syndrome (PCOS), a reproductive disorder in which cysts surround one's ovaries. This condition affects ovulation and the reproductive system while also increasing chances of Type 2 Diabetes and, in some instances, when tumors develop, Ovarian Cancer. Symptoms can range from anovulation to excessive facial hair growth. After undergoing several rounds of ultrasounds and lab work, the diagnosis was that both of my ovaries were enclosed with cysts and that my hormonal levels of testosterone were significantly elevated. A tumor was also detected but was later diagnosed as benign. However, I would have to deal with Type 2 Diabetes and the facial hair issue.

This was the beginning of another tiring journey, doctor to doctor, specialist to specialist. I was like, "Lord, how much more can I take?" The doctor decided that I should undergo an adrenal sampling to see precisely where the overproduction of hormones was coming from. After this test was completed, it was concluded that it was coming from the right adrenal gland. I would have to undergo another operation to have it removed. The day for surgery quickly arrived. Having been through this several times before, I was not nervous at all. The surgery went well. When getting back in my room, I was given too much pain medicine and began to show symptoms of cardiac arrest. The nurses rushed in quickly and made every attempt to stop this. After several minutes, things were back to normal, but that was a scare for everyone. I remained in the hospital for several days because my breathing and oxygen level were still not where they needed to be. After the surgery, I continued to have the same problem and was referred to an Endocrinologist. After running more tests, he discovered that the extra hormones were coming from my ovaries, not the adrenal gland.

On top of that, the reproductive specialist had noted in my chart that it was coming from the ovaries. Yes, I now found out they took out the wrong thing. The Endocrinologist began to treat me and stated that I might have to get my ovaries removed. Yet another trial, I may never be able to have the children that I always wanted. I was referred back to a different reproductive doctor who stated that I was too young to consider this procedure and that I could probably have children but would need to take medication or some form of treatment to do so. God had turned something else around for me.

DO NOT DEFINE YOURSELF BY YOUR PRESENT SITUATION

In April 2008, I decided that I wanted to go back to school to get my Master's Degree. Doing more soul searching, I wondered what I could major in. Always wanting to work with kids and give back to the Children's Hospital of the King's Daughters, I decided on Business Administration with a concentration in Healthcare Management. This way, I could use my Social Work degree and work in the healthcare field. Little did I know this decision was preparing me for something much more significant. In March 2009, I earned a Master's Degree and finished with straight A's and a 3.86 GPA. I was the first in my family on both sides to obtain a Master's Degree.

During this time in September 2008, I lost my Granny. My heart shattered into pieces, and I felt alone. Since I had become an introvert due to my experiences, I spent many days sitting and talking with her. While everyone else was happy out and about, I was most content sitting in the house with her. Grieving is definitely not easy, and the feeling never goes away, but I was happy to know that she was at peace.

In February 2009, I was laid off from my job. I thought it was the end of the world but knew in my mind that there had to be more to the story. My financial situation began to decline, healthcare bills were rising, and I just felt that my world was coming to an end; once again, anxiety started to set in. I ultimately decided to give up my apartment, move back home with my parents, and file bankruptcy.

Less than three weeks after being laid off, I got a call for a job interview. Could this be?? I am wondering who these people are and how did they find me. It was a job in the healthcare management field, and I was told they were looking for someone with strong administrative skills. I went in for the interview (which was the longest interview of my life), left nervous because it took so long, and received a call a few days later saying they wanted to offer me the job. Three weeks after being laid off, one week after finishing school, I landed a new job, making more than double what I previously made. Needless to say, it was definitely a financial blessing and what I needed at the time. What I thought was so bad turned out to be the best thing that ever happened to me. In my new career, I have advanced in several roles in a short period. I am provided with opportunities to excel, and they can pull from my strengths. But, most of all, it is a pleasant, Christian environment.

I knew this was definitely a God move. The President/CEO noticed something in me that I did not see in myself. I have very strong organizational, administrative, and planning skills; therefore, she recommended that I go for my Project Management certification. I had never heard of Project Management in my life, but this was definitely my passion!! Imagine being placed right in the middle of your passion and working in a place where you can exude passion and purpose. Every day I go to work, I am grateful. I no longer have those days when I felt I wasted all my skills and potential. I was even afforded the opportunity to co-chair our Community Giving Campaign and help the organization support other community organizations and help those in need.

In 2006, I began fellowshipping at a local church in the area. This church was all I ever dreamed of. It was not stuck on tradition, and it had an anointed leader with a nondenominational feel. In March 2009, I decided to become a part of this great ministry and let go of all the hurtful things I had endured. Since then, I have continued to see an increase. It does matter who you are connected to.

REALISTIC EXPECTATIONS

What do you expect of yourself? Do not measure yourself according to others' standards. Never expect to get what you give to people in return. Everyone is not you, and often people cannot give you what they do not have.

These are all lessons and things I wish I had applied much earlier in life because depression and anxiety are real!! Trying to live up to someone else's views and standards of you is not realistic. I have read that depression and anxiety are tough, but living with both is hell. And I have found this to be so true.

Through all of my experiences, of course, I would have to deal with this. There were often feelings of sadness and millions of times asking why is this happening to me. I used to question myself constantly, like what did I do to anyone? Am I cursed? Who or what am I suffering for? Something had to have happened for me to have been dealt such a hand in life. I would have to say that 2014 was probably the worst year for me. I spent days in bed. Usually, I could pull myself up and fake it until I make it, but this time I just could not. I could not fake a smile. I could not pretend that I was happy. I was just crushed inside. I tried to make myself keep going, but honestly, I was just existing and not living. The sun was shining outside many days, but I could not see it.

One day, I was just totally over it and ready to give up on everything, but I knew enough to cry out to God. At that point, that's all I could do. I had no strength, no will, no anything. I fell to my knees crying and praying, and from that day, my life slowly began to change. I had to encourage myself. I had to see myself where I wanted to be.

After that day, God began to show me that I was loved, and people began to love on me like never before (or so I thought). It was exactly what I needed at the moment. I remember that year being the best birthday ever. All of my friends were present. I think I had about six birthday parties because I decided it was time to celebrate me. I received flowers and tons of birthday cards. I know it was nothing but God touching the hearts of others to show that I was loved and valuable. I met someone who would become very special and a lifetime friend during this time. Unfortunately, we lost touch, but God never forgets, and He knows what you need.

I had good friends who made sure that I didn't stay down. Not only were they good friends, but friends of prayer and faith. One day, they invited me to the Daughters of Sarah conference. I remember the day so clearly and the message that broken bones do heal. This message spoke directly to me, so I knew I had to be attached to the messenger. The following year was a turning point for me. Desperate to love myself and boost self-confidence, I decided to join the Empowering Moments Mentoring Program. This was definitely a game-changer. Pastor Shavon always spoke to the broken pieces in me, and I always say to this day that she saved my life. I also formed a sisterhood with other ladies who could keep me lifted.

During this time and in the years to follow, I developed anxiety about everything. I heard the constant voice of others in my head saying, "You're too quiet," "You're a punk," "Why don't you speak up and be more vocal?" "You shouldn't avoid conflict." There were so many things, and of course, these things will weigh heavily on you because you feel you are being judged for who you are when no one knows your story or what made you that way. It was as if I was not good enough because I was so quiet and shy. So, yes, it certainly hurt, but I decided I would be me, take me or leave me.

Anxiety and depression come to destroy. If the devil has your mind, he has you, and I refused to be held hostage.

MAJOR LOSSES

I was blessed with a career that allowed me to travel. In 2016, I would travel to work in Baltimore, MD, every week. On one particular trip while away from home, I received a call at about 4:00 AM saying that my house was on fire. Yes, my brand new home I had just purchased one year prior. I heard the words, but I do not think they ever resonated with me. On an adrenaline rush, I hopped in my car at four in the morning and drove four hours back to Virginia, only to return to basically nothing. Everything I worked hard for was gone in the blink of an eye. Family and friends had arrived before I did, so everyone was already prepared for my reaction.

Surprisingly, I was very calm and did not shed a tear. Yes, I was devastated and dying on the inside, but I was totally numb to any kind of pain and emotion by this point in my life. I had just learned to trust God and go with the flow. I think the worst part of it for me was having to try to go through and salvage what I could because 95% of everything I ever owned was GONE. I had to start over. But even in the midst, God showed me a sign. While most of everything I had was destroyed, my Bible and anointing oil still stood on my nightstand, and I didn't lose any of my pictures or memories of my grandma. Everything else was replaceable, so I was thankful.

What do I do now, Lord?? Thankfully, I had insurance and many people who loved me and helped me recover. I got back way more than what I lost. I chose to live in a hotel for about a month just because I needed to regroup and process everything. After that, I stayed with family and friends and in a temporary apartment until I could rebuild my house. After almost a year of being without a place, I returned home.

What else could go wrong, right? Well, a couple of years after returning home, I began to experience random spotting. What could this be because it was very awkward? I always stayed current with doctor visits and had irregular cycles, so it was not too alarming for me. After several weeks, I decided to go to the doctor. After running several tests, she came back with surprising news. I was pregnant!! What?!?! I said, no, I'm not. Several days passed, and the bleeding did not subside, so I spent countless days at the hospital, only to discover that I was having a miscarriage. Unfortunately, the doctors did not offer any help but instead encouraged me just to let it bleed out. This was the most horrible feeling in my life!! Having to endure seeing that every day, knowing what my body was processing.

At my final appointment after the miscarriage, I had to have an ultrasound to ensure everything had cleaned out as it was supposed to. While looking at the screen, I noticed something!! There were no more cysts on my ovaries. While this whole experience was traumatizing, God made something good come out of it.

BACK AT IT AGAIN

In 2019, life was beginning to feel normal for me again. I was actively involved in church and finally found some peace and happiness until I woke up and could barely move one morning. Oh no!! What was this happening? For the next several months, I experienced excruciating pain in my back. Being the fighter I am, I tried to brush it off and push through, thinking this was just a phase.

Well, the phase didn't end. It got so bad to the point that I could not stand up and had to begin using a walker for assistance. Here I am at the age of 37, barely standing, using a walker, barely sitting or laying down, let alone moving. It was the worst pain I have ever experienced. God, this can't be life. Finally, I decided to see an orthopedic doctor. The initial diagnosis was that it might be a pinched nerve causing the pain, so steroid shots may help resolve the issue. I agreed and tried those because I was not too fond of the thought of having to do another surgery. As time passed, the pain did not subside. After more tests, it was discovered that the bone in the bottom of my spine had collapsed and was pushing on the sciatic nerve. This meant another back surgery.

I would have to undergo a few tests to prepare for the surgery, one being a spinal tap. In June 2019, I checked into the hospital for the test. I was nervous but feeling fine. The nurses checked all of my vitals, and everything was good. As they began to inject the dye into my spine, I could feel my head getting full as if I were about to pass out. I tried to communicate the feeling, but the next thing I knew, I had drifted away.

My spirit had transitioned to a different place!! I found myself in a big open white space face to face with an angel. It was a little girl dressed in all white with the most angelic presence. It was the most peaceful place ever, so I knew I was in the place between life and death. The angel guided me along the way, and it appeared as if I was at an intersection. She then said, "Do you want to come with me, or do you want to go back." I said, "No, I have to keep fighting; I have to get back to my girls." The next thing I knew, I woke up surrounded by a large team of doctors and nurses. Yes, I had coded!! It was like a movie, and I did not know what was happening. I remember them saying my pressure was moving back in the right direction and that I had initially gone into a seizure. I was rushed into the emergency room and hooked up to all kinds of machines to monitor my heart, lungs, and pulse. I remember shaking uncontrollably for about 15 minutes until my body finally calmed down. After completely coming around, I could see my mom crying and my pastor running into the room, so immediately, I am saying whatever happened could not have been good. I was a bit nervous, but my main concern was to assure them that I was okay. A few weeks later, I went in for another back surgery. They had to replace the bones at the bottom and reattach to my Harrington rod, but there was a totally different outcome this time, and everything went well. As a matter of fact, recovery was much quicker than anticipated.

In 2020, I would face multiple minor surgeries for Hidradenitis Suppurativa (also known as boils). If you have ever experienced this, then you know it is painful and uncomfortable. After one of the surgeries, I traveled to Atlanta to visit my aunt. When getting off the plane and going to the restroom, I noticed I was profusely bleeding. This wasn't a small amount of blood, but it was gushing and non-stop. My family called the airport paramedics, and as I was being wheeled through the airport, blood was just everywhere. Thinking that it was slowing down and stopping and just from the pressure of the airplane impacting the incision, we decided to make our way to the house. Well, it didn't stop, and my anxiety was rising. The paramedics were called, and I was rushed to the hospital. They checked me in, sat me in a wheelchair, wrapped a sheet around me, and let me sit there bleeding. This was not only embarrassing for me, but it was very traumatic not knowing what was going on. I was still bleeding, and almost four hours later, I was still just sitting in the emergency room because they were so backed up and told me I would just have to wait to be seen because it was not an emergency. While waiting, which ended up being probably over eight hours since initially starting, my blood sugar began to drop because I had not eaten. The nurses told my family not to give me anything because I may have to have emergency surgery. I kept saying I am going to pass out, and I think I may have briefly. My aunt rushed me to the nurse's station, and the nurse, with all of her strength, punched me directly in my chest. She then said, "See, she's fine." Was this really happening?? Like, where do they do this? I thought I had experienced a rough time with hospitals before, but this was the worst by far. After about ten hours, I was finally seen by the doctor. By that time, the bleeding had slowed, but I knew I had to have lost a few gallons of blood from my body that day.

THE PROMISE AFTER THE PRUNING

After the pruning, He will settle and establish you.

You must keep going even when you do not feel like it. Have you ever been in a place where everything seemed to go wrong? Well, guess what?!? You are not alone. I have been there too. But what happens when everything starts to go right?

I have the spiritual gift of prophecy; however, I am a prophetic dreamer, and God speaks to me through dreams. Well, for almost a year, I began to experience love in my dreams. It was a love like no other. I felt adored and cherished, and every morning I would awake after one of these dreams just in awe. It was just so surreal. It was a feeling that I always knew I wanted and deserved. For months, I could only see a silhouette of a person, but as time passed, God would show me more and more until He finally revealed it to me. Initially, I never acted upon these feelings and dreams, but eventually, I had to trust what God was showing me and take a leap of faith because surely I wasn't seeing and experiencing this for nothing.

Well, I will just say that it is incredible when your dreams are manifested, and you follow the voice of God. I prayed for someone for years, but God was waiting on me!! Now I am like, "Wow, God, you love me this much? You would do this for me?" What I thought He had taken from me years ago was restored. When you are in position, God will bless you. I had to be willing to give up some things to get what He had waiting for me all the time. I am doing it this time in God's way and His timing, and I know I will be blessed.

DO NOT DEFINE YOURSELF BY YOUR PAST

I could sit around and have a pity party for myself and talk about all the bad things I have endured, but it would not accomplish anything. I believe that something good comes out of everything bad that may happen. I had medical setbacks, but I am still here and have a story to tell. I was diagnosed with PCOS, but now instead of having one child at a time, I could have been blessed with multiples and only have to endure labor once. I lost my job, but now I have a better one. I filed for bankruptcy, but now my finances have increased, and I manage my money a lot better. In 12 years, my salary has more than doubled. In the year 2014, I was out of bankruptcy. In the year 2014, I was 32 years old. When I think of these numbers, one plus four is five, and three plus two is five. Five is the number of grace. God currently blesses me with his grace every day, but I expect a double portion of grace in the years to come.

Often I felt like Job, even to the point where I had to deal with boils, constantly wanting to throw in the towel, but I never turned my back on God. Now I am blessed beyond measure. Today I stand as a strong, young woman ready to face what life may bring my way and bless others whenever an opportunity presents itself. I am thankful for my trials and tribulations, grateful for the good that has come out of every situation, and thankful for God's strategic placement of others in my life. So when people say you can't do this or that, when people ask why you are the way you are, when people say why do you look like that, never be ashamed of your story, never be afraid to walk in your calling, and know that God's strength is made perfect in weakness. Life's situations come to mold you and shape you.

I DON'T LOOK LIKE WHAT I'VE BEEN THROUGH

I started writing this book in 2009 but got distracted. As I sit and think back, God was not finished with my story. Several years later, more obstacles and adversities have come along, but that greatest lesson of all is learning to love me. God now says it is finished. Share your story because it will reach millions and empower them to overcome and know that God makes all things possible. Sometimes it hurts to know that the people you give your heart to can't provide the same love in return, and as a result, you feel betrayed. During this process, no one knows what you personally have to endure. You sit and contemplate, "What did I do?" or "Why wasn't I good enough?" Empty feelings. Empty thoughts. Endless tears. I became silent. I lost my voice until one day, I came to a place where I was tired of being "THAT GIRL."

I was tired of being THAT GIRL who laid her heart on the line, giving so freely, letting people take advantage and trample upon it. I gave and gave of myself, only to end up empty, blinded to the fact that others could never love me the way I deserved. There were times when I was tired of being THAT GIRL who had no love left for herself because I trusted my heart with others, failing to realize that no one can care for your heart, your precious cargo, only God. I was tired of being THAT GIRL who cried herself to sleep, wondering who I was, why you're not worthy of love, and how did I get here. I was tired of being THAT GIRL who acted as a revolving door, letting others in and out, wanting to save them, feeling sorry for them when I needed to be saving myself. I was tired of being THAT GIRL who settled and forfeited my worth for others who did not know their own. I was tired of being THAT GIRL who was number two, three, or four when I always made others number one to me. I was tired of being THAT GIRL who believed lies and remained blind to manipulation, control, and jealousy. I was tired of being THAT GIRL who used others for my validation. I was tired of being THAT GIRL who smiled on the outside yet shed silent tears and died on the inside. I was tired of hiding behind the pain and residue of emotional and mental abuse. TIRED OF BEING THAT GIRL!!! But…..

I WILL BE THAT WOMAN!!!

THAT WOMAN who loves herself unconditionally; who understands that she is fearfully and wonderfully made. I will be THAT WOMAN who doesn't seek validation but understands that I am more than enough because I am made in the image of God. I will be THAT WOMAN who doesn't compromise her value, integrity, and dignity for someone who is not qualified. I will be THAT WOMAN who wakes up every day with a smile on her face and praise in her heart because I understand who I am and whose I am. I will be THAT WOMAN who isn't afraid to share her story because she knows she survived too much to qualify for this season. I will be THAT WOMAN who wakes up knowing that she is flawless and carries herself as such. I will be THAT WOMAN who walks with her head held high. I will be THAT WOMAN who waits for the one who God is preparing just for me. I will be THAT WOMAN who is set apart. I will receive the promise after the pain because there is greatness inside of me. I WILL BE THAT WOMAN!! Because I am a woman of grace, elegance, and worth, a woman of class and dignity, and a woman who refuses to settle!! I am THAT WOMAN who is more than enough!!

CONCLUSION

*E*veryone cannot go where God is trying to take you, and your story was explicitly designed for you. God knew us all when we were formed in our mother's womb and formed us each with purpose. He knew what we would endure before we even existed. Satan cannot hinder your progress or your destiny. You are valuable. I have shared my testimony, praying that it will bless others beyond measure because the blessings of the Lord are real. He makes us rich and adds no sorrow.

Hopefully, this will bless others and you as well. As I always say, I am constantly amazed at how awesome God is. There were days when the enemy tried to come in and attack me and hinder my destiny, but I refused to let him do so. In my alone time and talking to God, he told me to share a little bit of my story to bless someone else because we are overcome by our testimony. By no means is this meant to boast or brag, but simply to share how good God is and how the size of our storms determines the magnitude of our blessings.

God is always protecting and preparing us for so much greater. God says touch not my anointed and do my prophet no harm. At the age of 40, I can say I am a strong, independent woman. Everything I went through has made me who I am. I hold a Bachelor's Degree, a Master's Degree, and a Project Management Certification. I am the youngest person in a senior leadership role at my job and well above my dream salary. I am a homeowner. I will be debt-free very soon. I was in a relationship for over 15 years, and when I decided to let go, I lost absolutely NOTHING, but gained A LOT!!! I have a wealth of friends and family. Anytime I even think of giving up, God sends me a sign and lets me know everything is working for my good. I often don't recognize my strength, but I always find joy in blessing and encouraging others. Hopefully, you will pass this on and be a blessing to someone and encourage them that this too shall pass. When you have so many "no's" from everyone, all you need is one YES from God. Believe in yourself, love yourself and be responsible for yourself. Find joy in your journey. Remember, everyone has a story and is fighting some battle. Be Blessed!!

AFFIRMATION

I declare that this day I am free.

God has set me free, and I will stay free.

I will move forward and not look back.

I am not my past; those issues were only ingredients to my destiny.

I do not look like what I've been through.

I am beautiful, strong, bold, humble, blessed, and healed.

I am more than a conqueror; I am an overcomer.

Setback or Setup: Trusting God's Process For Your Life
Sherita Green

I will not walk in fear, but I will walk boldly in my calling.

I am what God says I am.

My emotions will not master me, but my emotions will be servants to get me to my destiny.

I will walk with purpose and receive everything that God has for me.

I survived too much to qualify for this season.

I will associate myself with who I want to become.

I will not walk in darkness; I will be a light to others.

I have strong faith; therefore, I will have a strong finish.

I am not worthless; I must be earned.

I see myself in the future; I am called to greatness.

I will receive the promise after the pain.

I can do whatever I set my mind to and achieve my goals.

I forgive those who have mistreated me and did not recognize my worth.

I am not a victim; I am a victor.

I trust the process, and I will survive!!

THE SCARS

The scars that I have remind me that I have endured some things,

That no matter what the circumstance, I can overcome what life may bring.

The scars I have serve a purpose to people I see each day,

Letting them know that God is real and He always makes a way.

Some say I am imperfect or that I don't look the norm,

Setback or Setup: Trusting God's Process For Your Life
Sherita Green

I say that it's a testament that I have endured my storm.

Some say I am too quiet or that I'm just too shy,

I say if you read my story, then you would understand why.

Some say that I'm too generous and that I give my all,

I say when you've been blessed like me; you want to catch others when they fall.

The scars that I have remind me wherever I may go,

That the scars I have are nothing compared to the one who sits on high and looks below

Just a reminder today that God is greater than your circumstances, and EVERYTHING in life serves a purpose. You are fearfully and wonderfully made, and God makes no mistakes.

REFERENCE

"Transformation." *What is Transformation in the Bible?* (9 March 2021). Retrieved from https://blog.biblesforamerica.org/what-is-transformation-in-the-bible/#:~:text=First%2C%20let%E2%80%99s%20look%20at%20how%20the%20Merriam-Webster%20dictionary,a%20major%20change%20and%20ends%20up%20looking%20different.

www.ingramcontent.com/pod-product-compliance
Lightning Source LLC
Chambersburg PA
CBHW062141100526
44589CB00014B/1651